AGILITY
DOGS

BY MARIE PEARSON

CANINE
ATHLETES

SportsZone

An Imprint of Abdo Publishing
abdobooks.com

abdobooks.com

Published by Abdo Publishing, a division of ABDO, PO Box 398166, Minneapolis, Minnesota 55439. Copyright © 2019 by Abdo Consulting Group, Inc. International copyrights reserved in all countries. No part of this book may be reproduced in any form without written permission from the publisher. SportsZone™ is a trademark and logo of Abdo Publishing.

Printed in the United States of America, North Mankato, Minnesota
092018
012019

Cover Photo: E. Cummings/iStockphoto
Interior Photos: Mary Altaffer/AP Images, 5, 7, 29; Shutterstock Images, 8; James Brey/iStockphoto, 11; GoDog Photo/Shutterstock Images, 13; Pat Jarrett/The Daily News Leader/AP Images, 14–15; Joe Giddens/PA Wire URN:32352592/Press Association/AP Images, 19; Christian Mueller/Shutterstock Images, 21; Timothy A. Clary/AFP/Getty Images, 25; A. Mirsberger/Tierfotoagentur/Alamy, 27

Editor: Patrick Donnelly
Series Designer: Craig Hinton

Library of Congress Control Number: 2018949078

Library of Congress Cataloging-in-Publication Data

Names: Pearson, Marie, author.
Title: Agility dogs / by Marie Pearson.
Description: Minneapolis, Minnesota : Abdo Publishing, 2019 | Series: Canine athletes | Includes online resources and index.
Identifiers: ISBN 9781532117367 (lib. bdg.) | ISBN 9781641855938 (pbk) | ISBN 9781532170225 (ebook)
Subjects: LCSH: Dog sports--Juvenile literature. | Agility trials for dogs--Juvenile literature. | Dogs--Behavior--Juvenile literature.
Classification: DDC 636.70887--dc23

TABLE OF
CONTENTS

AGILITY FAME

Jessica Ajoux was playing tug with her Border collie, Fame(US)—pronounced *famous*—just outside of the agility ring. It was the 2018 Masters Agility Championship at the Westminster Kennel Club dog show. Ajoux hoped that she and Fame(US), also called Fame, could beat the current leader. Carly, a golden retriever, had run the course in 38.14 seconds. The crowd clapped as the announcer called Ajoux and Fame into the ring. Fame barked with excitement.

Many breeds and mixes compete at Westminster's Masters Agility Championship.

Ajoux told Fame to stay and then walked past the first jump. At Ajoux's cue, Fame launched forward and sailed over a series of jumps. She ran up the seesaw and paused just a moment as it tipped down. Then she was off again, flying over more jumps and sprinting as Ajoux guided her to each obstacle. The crowd erupted as she raced over the final two jumps and leaped into Ajoux's arms in celebration. The announcer shouted, "Just shattered the time set by Carly! Over 8.5 seconds faster!"

A few more dogs followed after Fame. None of them beat her time. Ajoux and Fame had won the Masters Agility Championship.

AGILITY HISTORY

Dog agility is a popular sport around the world. Handlers run dogs through an obstacle course. The goal is to finish the course in the fastest time with no mistakes. It requires both speed and agility.

AGILITY ON TELEVISION

The Masters Agility Championship isn't the biggest agility trial. But it is one of the few that people can watch on television. The winners get a lot of media attention. Ajoux gave many interviews after she and Fame won.

Jessica Ajoux and Fame show off their ribbons at the 2018 Westminster Kennel Club Dog Show.

The sport began in the United Kingdom in 1977. Crufts Dog Show organizers were looking for a way to fill the space between events at a dog show. They created a jumping event. They based it on show jumping for

Although the obstacles may look similar, the way people have trained their dogs for and run in agility trials has changed a lot over the decades.

horses. It also had a tunnel, a ramp to climb over, and other obstacles. In 1978 at Crufts, two teams of four dogs competed against each other. The crowd loved it.

Dog clubs quickly picked it up as a sport. They created rules and invented and improved on obstacles. The sport soon spread to the United States and other countries. The courses have gone from simple figure-eight patterns to mazes of twists and turns. People and dogs around the world compete in local, national, and international events. Others train just for fun. Handlers love the competition. They love the speed and excitement. They enjoy meeting others who love their dogs. And they love the bond it creates between dog and handler.

RULES
OF THE GAME

Agility can seem a bit confusing to someone watching for the first time. There are many different obstacles and rules. Both influence how a dog scores.

Jumps are one of the most common obstacles. Some are simple, single-bar jumps. Others might be two or three single-bar jumps set close together. The dog has to clear these in one leap. Bar jumps encourage dogs to jump high. Broad jumps require them to jump far. The dog clears a row of boards in one bound. The tire jump is a circular obstacle. Dogs leap through the center.

Some obstacles such as the A-frame are high off the ground.

Most courses have tunnels that the dogs run through. Some have a table. The dog jumps on the table and stays there for five seconds.

Three obstacles are called contact obstacles. The A-frame is two wide panels set end to end. The ends meet in a peak, like a capital *A*. Dogs run up one side and down the other. The dog walk has three panels that are 1 foot (30 cm) wide. The middle panel is propped up and runs parallel with the ground. The other two panels form ramps up to and down from the middle. The dog runs up one ramp, across the middle, and down the other ramp. The seesaw is also a 1-foot (30 cm) wide panel. It is similar to a seesaw at a playground. One end rests on the ground. A dog runs up that end and then slows or stops after the halfway point. This tips the high end to the floor, and the dog finishes the run down. Each contact obstacle has a yellow section on both ends. A dog has to put at least one paw in the yellow section as it finishes the obstacle.

Weave poles are usually a set of six or 12 poles. The poles are arranged in a straight line. They stick up from a base. A dog must enter the weave poles between the first

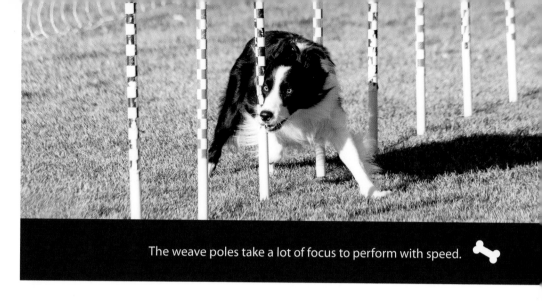
The weave poles take a lot of focus to perform with speed.

two poles. The first pole is at the dog's left shoulder. It weaves left and right through the rest of the poles.

CLUBS AND CLUB RULES

Dog agility clubs are popular in the United States, and individual clubs offer different services. The American Kennel Club (AKC) and United Kennel Club (UKC) keep records of purebred dogs. They also organize various events including agility. Other clubs do only agility trials. These include the North American Dog Agility Council (NADAC) and the United States Dog Agility Association (USDAA).

Agility clubs have slightly different rules, depending on their unique combination of obstacles. A standard agility course uses many obstacles. But some courses might

AGILITY
COURSE

TIRE

WEAVE POLES

TUNNEL

focus on one particular obstacle, such as tunnels or jumps. In most courses, the obstacles are numbered by the order in which each dog must clear them. Other courses might also have obstacles arranged on the field, but handlers pick which to use and in what order. For these courses, handlers try to get a certain number of points or combination of obstacles.

JUMP

SEESAW

JUDGE

Agility handlers aim to qualify in each course they run. This means they must finish a course with at least the minimum score required. A perfect score might be 100. Dogs can lose points if, for example, they leave the table too soon. Running past an obstacle or taking on the wrong obstacle can also cost points. Each course has a standard course time. Handlers try to finish the course in this time or faster. They lose points for every second longer it takes to finish. If a dog loses too many points, it is disqualified.

Some mistakes result in an automatic nonqualifying score (NQ). In AKC, missing the yellow section of an obstacle is an NQ. So is dropping a bar on a jump. In UKC and other clubs, if a handler touches an obstacle or the dog on purpose, that is also an NQ.

In addition to course rules, clubs feature different levels of competition. Courses vary in difficulty. Some levels are good for dogs new to trialing. AKC's Novice and NADAC's Intro courses are typical levels for beginners. Higher levels get gradually harder. They allow for fewer mistakes. AKC's Premier and NADAC's Elite levels are much more difficult. Dogs and handlers are highly trained.

COMPETITION

Dogs compete against other dogs in the same level. They also compete against dogs of similar height. These are called height classes. Height determines how high the jumps are. In AKC, dogs more than 14 inches (36 cm) and up to 18 inches (46 cm) at the shoulder must clear jumps that are 16 inches (41 cm) in height.

During qualifying runs, dogs are scored in their level and height class. They can get first, second, third, or fourth place for the fastest, cleanest runs. They can also get titles. Titles are letters that go before or after a dog's name. These letters indicate an important achievement. In AKC, a dog that has three qualifying runs on standard Novice courses gets the Novice Agility title. The letters *NA* are added to the dog's name.

There are many agility rules. It is important for handlers to know the rules before they compete. But even more important is having a well-trained dog.

WHICH CLUB?

Handlers may pick clubs with rules or courses that work best for them and their dogs. AKC courses don't always have a lot of space between obstacles. Dogs need to handle sharp turns. USDAA courses, where speed is most important, have a lot of space between obstacles.

TRAINING A CHAMPION

Dogs of all breeds and mixes compete and win in agility. But some are known for being especially talented. Border collies and Shetland sheepdogs often win at trials around the world. Both breeds like to work hard. They are smart, trainable, and have lots of energy, so they usually finish courses quickly. Golden retrievers, standard and miniature poodles, and papillons also excel at agility.

But any type of dog can compete. Even dogs that are independent-minded or low-energy can succeed. Agility can give confidence to otherwise timid dogs. Training is

Poodles can make smart and speedy agility dogs.

the biggest key to a great agility dog. Before beginning training, it's important to make sure the dog is healthy. Dogs with joint issues can get injured easily. It might not be safe for them to compete. Dogs with thick, heavy coats or with short noses can overheat quickly. These dogs can still compete in agility. But handlers need to know when to pause and cool them down.

STARTING YOUNG

Many dogs begin training as puppies. They should not do most agility obstacles until they are done growing to prevent injury. But puppies can learn skills that help them become agility stars. Many people take their puppies to puppy classes. Socialization is important. This means getting puppies used to being around lots of people and dogs. They should be comfortable with strange or unexpected noises. Agility trials are busy and noisy. Puppies should also learn to walk on different surfaces such as bubble wrap or wobbly boards. This gives them confidence to walk over contact obstacles.

Learning to sit and stand on wobbly objects improves an agility dog's balance.

Puppies learn to come when called. They run agility off leash, so responding to this command keeps them safe. They also learn where their bodies are. Skills such as backing up, putting all four feet in a small box, or lifting each foot on command teach them where their feet are. These skills also build balance. Body awareness helps keep dogs from falling off tall obstacles.

Most importantly, puppies learn training is fun. Sessions should be short and exciting. Food and toys make great rewards. If a puppy makes a mistake, trainers take the lesson back a step. They set the puppy up for success. This gives puppies confidence and makes them excited to work.

LEARNING THE OBSTACLES

Once they're done growing, dogs can start learning obstacles. It is important to train with an agility instructor. This person knows how to teach dogs to do obstacles safely.

Tunnels start short. Dogs get treats or toys for running through them. Gradually the tunnel gets longer as the dog gains confidence. Contact obstacles start low to the ground. Dogs often learn to slow down or stop at the end. This way they don't jump off before touching the yellow zone. Obstacles are raised gradually until they are at the full height.

Once a dog knows how to do the obstacles, the instructor or handler can start putting obstacles together.

MASSAGES

Canine massages can help keep dogs flexible. They can also help dogs relax. Many professional agility trainers, including Susan Garrett, bring their dogs to massage therapists who specialize in dogs.

They start with just a few in a row. Handlers encourage the dogs to run quickly. They make sure the dog has fun.

STAYING HEALTHY

It is important to keep agility dogs healthy. Keeping dogs at a healthy weight is important. Overweight dogs are more likely to injure their joints. Nails should be kept short. Long nails can tear or cause sore feet. Regular exercise keeps dogs strong to perform obstacles safely.

Handlers should never run a dog that is limping or ill. Handlers should warm up their dogs before practicing agility or running a course. They should cool down the dogs after. Warming up can include walking, stretching, spinning in circles, and backing up. These exercises help a dog's muscles become flexible and ready for exercise. Cooling down typically just involves slow walking. Cooling down keeps muscles from cramping.

It takes a lot of training to get ready for an agility trial. Trainers are always learning more about how to keep dogs safe and happy. All this work pays off at a trial.

COMPETITION
DAY

As the day of a trial approaches, the club hosting the trial sends out the order of classes. An AKC trial might begin with Open Jumpers, then Novice Jumpers, Open Standard, and Novice Standard. Some clubs also send the order of all the dogs in the classes. Agility teams who run in the later classes can come to the trial later. But some have to be there for the very first class, which may start at 8:00 a.m.

Handlers arrive sometime before their class. They set up kennels and chairs in designated areas. Some people

Some handlers rub their dogs' muscles to help them warm up before a trial.

have fans and mats that help keep their dogs cool. They make sure their dogs have water.

There is usually one judge for a trial. When a course is ready, all handlers gather in the ring. The trial judge goes over a few rules. Then everyone has a set time to walk the course. In NADAC, handlers have five minutes to do this. When walking the course, handlers memorize which obstacles they will do and in what order. They look at the course through their dogs' eyes. They look for obstacles their dogs might attempt that they aren't supposed to. Then they figure out how to make sure their dogs take the right obstacles. They figure out what signals they need to give their dogs to finish the course cleanly and quickly.

Handlers warm up their dogs shortly before their runs. They enter the ring as the competitor before them finishes. The handler sets up the dog by the first obstacle and takes off its leash. At the judge's signal, the handler releases the dog to start running. Many courses have

TRIAL LOCATION

Trials may be held at dog training facilities with cushioned mats. They might be at indoor sports arenas on artificial turf. Some might be outdoors on grass. Other trials are held in barns with dirt floors.

Handlers of all ages can train and compete in agility.

sensors at the first and last obstacle. These sensors start and stop the clock, giving the dog's exact time on the course. The judge follows the team but stays out of its way. He or she notes any errors.

The team might celebrate at the end of the run by jumping or playing tug with the leash. The handler quickly leashes the dog and leaves the ring to cool off. Once the dog is cooled off, the handler typically puts the dog back in its crate to wait for their next class.

VOLUNTEERING

Trials rely on volunteers. Handlers often volunteer during classes their dogs aren't entered in. Visitors can also volunteer. Some people help build courses. They use maps to move obstacles where they need to be for the next class. Some are bar setters. If a dog knocks down a jump bar, they set it back up. They also set bars higher or lower as a class moves from one height to another. Leash runners sit near the first obstacle. They grab the leash when a dog starts running. They take it quickly to the exit gate so the handler can leave the ring right after the run.

Gate stewards make sure the next dog is ready at the gate. Scribes watch the judge. The judge notes errors with hand signals. The scribe writes down each signal. Volunteering is a great way to learn the rules of agility. It's also a good way to watch the canine athletes up close.

SCORING

Scores are posted sometime after the class is finished. Score sheets note who qualified and if they placed first, second, third, or fourth. Dogs get ribbons and rosettes for

Whether or not a team won or even qualified, it's always important to celebrate each run.

qualifying and for placing. Some might get a prize such as a dog toy. Only a few large trials have prize money. Most people compete for the ribbons and titles.

Agility is a fun and exciting sport. It is a great way for people to bond with their dogs and get exercise. Handlers often make many friends as they train and compete. And dogs prove how amazingly athletic they can be.

GLOSSARY

agility
The ability to move quickly and easily.

breed
Domestic animals that have common ancestors and physical and behavioral traits.

canine
Dog.

club
A group of people who take memberships and organize dog events.

cramp
The act of a muscle tightening and becoming hard or painful to use.

joint
The point where two parts of a skeleton are joined and can bend, such as the elbow.

media
Journalists, reporters, and other people who broadcast the news.

parallel
Lying in the same direction.

qualify
To have met all of the requirements in a run so that the run counts toward a placement.

rosette
A ribbon with a round, ruffled badge at the top.

trial
An event where dogs compete, are judged, and receive scores.

MORE INFORMATION

ONLINE RESOURCES

Booklinks
NONFICTION NETWORK
FREE! ONLINE NONFICTION RESOURCES

To learn more about agility, visit **abdobooklinks.com**. These links are routinely monitored and updated to provide the most current information available.

BOOKS

Furstinger, Nancy. *Dogs*. Minneapolis, MN: Abdo Publishing, 2014.

Furstinger, Nancy. *Herding Dogs*. Minneapolis, MN: Abdo Publishing, 2019.

Sundance, Kyra. *101 Dog Tricks, Kids Edition: Fun and Easy Activities, Games, and Crafts*. Beverly, MA: Quarry, 2014.

INDEX

ABOUT THE AUTHOR

Marie Pearson is a children's book author and editor. She has trained two dogs in agility, and she competes with her standard poodle in agility and several other dog sports.